Spotli...

NEW DAWN

Edited by

Neil Day & Sarah Andrew

For
Jenny and family
Hope this is the beginning
of better things

love

(Mum).

First published in Great Britain in 2001 by
SPOTLIGHT POETS
Remus House, Coltsfoot Drive,
Peterborough, PE2 9JX
Telephone (01733) 898102
Fax (01733) 313524

SB ISBN 1 84077 058 9

FOREWORD

As a nation of poetry writers and lovers, many of us are still surprisingly reluctant to go out and actually buy the books we cherish so much. Often when searching out the work of newer and less known authors it becomes a near impossible mission to track down the sort of books you require. In an effort to break away from the endless clutter of seemingly unrelated poems from authors we know nothing or little about; Spotlight Poets has opened up a doorway to something quite special.

New Dawn is a collection of poems to be cherished forever; featuring the work of eleven captivating poets each with a selection of their very best work. Placing that alongside their own personal profile gives a complete feel for the way each author works, allowing for a clearer idea of the true feelings and reasoning behind the poems.

The poems and poets have been chosen and presented in a complementary anthology that offers a variety of ideals and ideas, capable of moving the heart, mind and soul of the reader.

Neil Day & Sarah Andrew

CONTENTS

Michael L Waldron

Born January 1st 1943 in the City of Plymouth, Devon spending most of my youth exploring the wilderness of Dartmoor, taking an interest in and developing a love for nature. Educated at Plympton Grammar school near Plymouth my interest in the sciences drew me away from the more artistic pursuits, although these remained as hobbies.

Pursuing a career in psychiatric nursing I witnessed some of the torment a sick mind can bring. This influenced some of my subsequent poems. On the closure of the large hospital in which I was employed I entered the private sector nursing homes for the elderly, here another facet of the ageing mind was experienced.

Always having an interest in the unexplained and unseen I became a founding member of a mystery group studying mythology and world religions, adding to a growing variety of themes found in my writings.

I find that putting pen to paper or fingers to keyboard are an efficient way of abreacting the numerous stresses and trials of everyday survival and is a more satisfying method of relieving turbulent innermost feelings, once expressed on paper these seem to have less impact and can be dealt with more easily.

Within my writings can be found elements of romance, depression and the magical symbolism of myth and legend. Writing poetry can be tidal and inspiration ebbs and flows at the whim of the muses, a single word or action, a scenic view, all these can bring the poetry surging to the surface of the mind. I would not presume to say that I have any particular poetic style but simply channel (to use a current expression) the words onto the page.

TEARS OF THE MOON

I stood upon a hilltop high, last night
and watched a rising moon ascend
across a spangled cloak, of stars.
Its face of beaten silver shone, and yet,
a nebulous trace of dark I spied.
I gazed and gazed yet could not see
what caused this darker thing which marred
the beauty of the moon.

But as she rose to higher arc
a drop of brighter silver shone
upon her cheek. A single tear
which, tumbling down from heaven's heights
I caught with outstretched hand
a tear which spoke of sadness deep
of things unsaid and wounded heart.

And raising to my lips this fragile gem
upon it placed a tender kiss
in hope to mend the hurt.
Then high I tossed it with a prayer
and watched it soar with comet's grace
returning there from whence it fell
to turn from silver sadness cold
with magic charm to joy of gold.

And on the hilltop high I vowed
that ever need should be
those tears could fall upon my hand
and blessed would I be.
I left the lonely hilltop high
to wend my way along the path
and overhead that glorious moon
with moonbeams lit my way.

PHONETIC HEAVEN?

The scalpel of my voice
carves the silence into patterns.
Sentences fall from my lips to
blow amidst the leaves of winter,
dry and withered upon the frozen ground.

Between that which is spoken
lie the unsaid truths, behind
them, motives, rank on rank
driving speech onwards and outwards
assaulting the unwary ear.

And once released upon the outer world
nought can bring them back.
Where do they go to, these dancing ones
these subtle vibrations of flesh and chord?
Is there a graveyard of conversations?

Perhaps in some great noise rent place
all that was ever spoken, circles,
round and round with none to hear.
A place which never knows the stillness
of silence.

SOFTLY IN THE NIGHT

The candle flickers, burning low, and he,
with eyes now weary lays his quill aside
surveys the room and window dark
and there upon the dampened glass
as if spectator to his work. A moth
its amber eyes reflecting candle flame.

Within his mind a gentle voice, enquiring,
he softly slides the casement wide,
into the room on burnished wings it flies
but not as any moth would do
dash to the flame and death
but settles close beside his quill.

The window closed against the night
again he takes his seat, and leaning back
with half closed lids, surveys the tiny life
and slowly there the tiny moth
takes on a different shape
a maiden fair with gleaming hair and eyes of deepest brown.

A robe of finest silk adorns her comely frame
and on her head a diadem of opals flash with light
she speaks, and, with her words inspire
such visions magic only could evoke
transfixed, enchanted, transported far
to leafy glades where in the cool green light
a pool of crystal water lies.

Within its depths the great carp swirl
and speak of secrets old
an ancient cup beside the pool
taken by the maiden's hand and filled
he drinks and in the drinking of
awakes. The candle cold and dead.

A dream? Perhaps or maybe not.
Only the moth could tell.

TELLING

I tell of my love for thee
within the dark caverns of the earth.
Where dwarfs and gnomes dwell
where mineral and crystals sleep.

I tell of my love for thee
upon the high hills and mountains.
Where hawk and eagle soar
where the wind flies and free.

I tell of my love for thee
in the green meadows and valleys.
Where the silver rivers wend their way
and golden trout flash, leaping high.

I tell of my love for thee
in the hot dust of the desert.
Where burning sun scorches down
on winding camel trains.

I tell of my love for thee
among the stars and wandering ones.
Where comets flash across the infinite
and meteors their brief life give.

I tell of my love for thee
beyond the boundaries of time and space.
Where lie the secrets unrevealed
and thoughts take shape and form.

And I unceasingly shall tell
of my true love for thee.
Knowing in my heart and soul
thou also lovest me.

LOVE'S GARDEN

Wilt thou walk with me in the garden of my love?
For I will deck thee with all the flowers of spring
wash thee in the waters of the crystal stream
and warm thee with the sun of my own soul.

Upon the softest moss thou shalt recline.
I'll thread sweet grasses 'mongst thy silken maiden hair
trace patterns of eternity upon thy skin
and press thy lips with fragrant kiss.

Embracing close shall I a fire ignite
which, rising high, shall both consume
in tide of passion o'erflowing time
till all is nought and nought is all.

And in its embers shall we lie
two souls, one breath upon the wind.
To dream a single dream
and thus to be forever.

Oh! Say that thou wilt walk with me
and I shall weave a cloak
of rainbow light and blackbird song.
to keep thee from the chill.

A bower of roses wild I'll make
and there thou shalt take rest.
Wild honey touched with moonbeams glow
I'll find for thee to feast.

A cup of rich red wine I'll bring
from light of setting sun
but more than this I'll give to thee
my love for evermore.

THUNDERHEADS

Out of the still air they come
building across the sky.
Dark and menacing
casting shadows across field and wood
the silence grows tangible
waiting in anticipation.

Still they grow, taking sustenance
from the moisture of a million lungs
the outflung breath of plant and animal.
Deep within their power grows
forming and reforming.
Strength and strength.

Flashing bolts they fling,
lighting the earth
bringing fire and tumult.
Their voices grumbling and cracking
shake the mountains.
Thunderheads making war.

Wizards of Storm wield jagged wands
filled with nature's power.
Unleashing raw energy,
lashing the earth.
Cleansing.
Renewing.

CAVALRY OF THE MOON

Thundering on they come, pennants flying wild, torn.
The Moon cavalry, charging.
Hurling themselves against the bulwarks stone,
leaping high to crash upon the land beyond.
Giving their all to reclaim what was lost.
On and on they come, unceasingly.
These troops who answer to her power.
And high behind them she, implacable,
her face gold tinted in the west
watching her minions battle.
And she enlists the aid of him
whose breathing spurs them on.
Unceasingly advancing rank and file
down the silver path.
But slowly as the Earth turns on
her armies face a different shore
to battle there anew.
Yet soon the time shall come
when she, standing before the Lord
shall overshadow him and wear his crown.
Then shall her armies march
with lances couched and sharp
to take the land by storm,
and shall stretch her limbs
at that shrill trumpet blast
to rid herself with fire
of that persistent itch of Man.

TRUE MUSIC OF THE NIGHT AND DAY

Come softly to me when the sun has set.
Come gently to me in the starlight's glow
clothed in a silver garment of moonbeams
and I shall enfold you in my arms
and draw from you such sweet music
that would halt the passing time
bewitching all who hear.

Come swiftly to me when the sun is born.
Come running to me as dawn's fair hand
sweeps far the shades of night.
Clothed in the golden rays of another day
and I will paint for you images
that would blind the mind
and make imagination dull and drab.

Come slowly to me in the noonday heat.
Come sinuous as crimson snake
to coil about my breast.
Clothed in a robe of orange flame
and I will raise a fire within
to scorch the novan fires
and make them seem as ice.

Come then to me as dusk descends.
Come to me with sleep-dimmed eyes.
Clothed in the sheerest silk
and I will soothe your troubled thoughts,
with kiss, caress and word
that you will sleep in paradise, with me.

UNTITLED

Tearing into the abyss of ecstasy, diving deep into that unknown place
that place where all things dissolve and become as no thing.
I will fill thee with the power of fire,
the realms of mankind fading into a mist of unknowing.
I shall rend and tear thee into myself, yet within thee shall I be lost,
struggling against the current of that stream which is irresistible.
Scream loud my love for the gateway to the darkness yawns wide.
Call softly my love before the gatekeeper of joy,
he whose hand is as a closed fist against your heart.
I yearn for the escape itself into a maelstrom of pieces from the tree,
floating to spiral down into the darker depths beneath.
The image changes, swirls from one to another, many in one.
I know not which, pounding through the red mists of the heart.
Sing for me oh black hooded bird,
peck out my eyes that I may not see the path into the joy and light.
The sun warms my bones and brings the dawn of other days.
But still the trembling of the earthen bank,
spills from the cup the wine of peace.
I stand with foot upon your neck. Defeated.
The clock ticks on.

Leslie Loader

Leslie Thomas Loader born 1923 in Southampton, served in the Army (The Hampshire Regiment, later the Royal Hampshire Regiment) twice during the 1939/45 war. In May 1939, at the age of 16 years and 1 month, he joined the Territorial Army by stating he was 18. 'Joining the 'Terriers' was one of the best things that I have done' he claims. It is the best Youth Club for any teenager and should be expanded now to give the youth of today the sense of purpose that the 'Terriers' gave to us.

He was mobilised in August 1939 but discharged for a 'misstatement of age on enlistment' in December. Joining the Local Defence Volunteers (later the Home Guard) as soon as they were formed he was a Sergeant at 18. He was 'needed again at 18½' and was commissioned in the County Regiment.

As a young officer he saw active service in Italy, was wounded and after five months in hospital in North Africa and several months of sick leave in England was discharged with a pension at 21.

In 1947, he started a lifetime of unpaid public service, first as a Southampton Councillor, then in the 1955 General Election he stood for Parliament as the Conservative and National Liberal Candidate for his home constituency of Southampton Itchen.

Later in 1962, he formed a Charitable Housing Society that provides sheltered accommodation now for about 450 elderly people in the Southampton area. In 1980, largely for this, he was made a Commander of the Order of the British Empire.

In 1987, he was Knighted largely for services to the Health Services. Leslie Loader, like so many of his generation, was very affected by his war experiences and still suffers nightmares. Some of his war experiences are expressed in his prose poems.

AFTER THE BATTLE . . . TIME IS SHORT!

And then one slips between the dream and memory real,
That in one's brain released and lives again,
The aftermath of terror and of noise,
The eerie silence broken only by the Wounded's moans,
And quiet talking of them to the ones they love,
Mother, Wife . . . no time for Floozies now,
Mum, Mum, I love you Mum,
Darling dearest Wife my love, look after Jimmy please,
And God please help my lovely wife, with him,
And then an enemy or a former one, for there are none,
Among the wounded now,
Who speaks his words with German tongue that means the same!
Mum, Mum, I love you Mum, and so the silence broken,
By the pleas, for time is short and getting shorter still,
The cry, please help me, please, is the call,
Stretcher-bearers, stretcher-bearers, where are you? Help me please,
And stretcher-bearers bravely do their job,
Some would not fight, religiously opposed to killing, but,
Just as brave as those who do and so God's work they undertake,
Of Help and Mercy all and seeing blood and guts the worst of all,
That they never will be able to forget,
Stretcher-bearers, stretcher-bearers, where are you?
Please help me; Help me please . . . all weaker now,
The talking's less as the wounded leaves the field of battle
in their different ways,
And later still, much later, later still,
The farmer tills the soil that has a memory too,
Of how man used it, nay abused it,
In such an awful, awful way!

THE LONG, LONG DAY

The day after we crossed the River Volturno in October 1943 was perhaps the longest day of my life. Of course, it had twenty-four hours in it just like every other day but we were tired and our Sister Battalion on our right had been savagely mauled and we had not been able to help them, which made it worse. We also knew that we had the walking through a minefield to look forward to as soon as our friend the darkness came to hide us. In the meanwhile we lay still in the open and dared not move for fear of a sniper's bullet!

In friendly rushes where we lay, our enemies were two,
the usual one and the light all day.
It was to be a long, long day.

Then came the order, move forward to be open,
then unprotected, that made if three but we dared not say.
It was to be a trying, long, long day.

Moved by orders firmly given, to into the open we were bidden,
from our friendly rushes, where we were hidden.
It was to be a trying, nerve tearing, long, long day!

To in the open, was it sense? We were nervous but we went
for we knew from the single shots we heard,
the sniper's bullet that we feared.
It was to be a trying, nerve tearing, awful, long, long day.

In the open we could be seen and from the single shot, we often heard,
we knew we would be sighted if we moved, by the sniper to us unseen.
All through this trying, nerve tearing, awful, scary, long, long day.

So behind a little mound we found that became our cosy friend,
We hid ourselves as best we could, as any well trained soldier would
All through this trying, nerve tearing, awful, scary, rotten,
long, long day.

So all day long we had the strain,
Were we in the sniper's sights and aim?
All through this long, long day.

WE BURIED HIM IN HIS FORMER HOME!

No drum, no flag, no service said,
We did our best,
He knew we would,
He was our friend,
But he was shot,
And on his body,
We did not want,
The flies,
To enjoy their little games,
So,
We rolled him in,
To the weapon slit,
That was his home,
Until he ventured out,
And,
Was shot,
That brought his end.

BUY A POPPY? YOU DON'T SEE WHY YOU SHOULD!

(Written in memory of my comrade and friend Charlie Chainey late of the Royal Hampshire Regiment, who has gone now. He left us covered by the Union Flag, Flanked by Draped Standards, proudly held by comrades with a spray of Minden Roses. But he is just waiting and hoping to meet us again soon.)

Those serving in the Royal Hampshire Regiment commemorate the Battle of Minden of 1759 by wearing the Minden Rose on the first of August each year.

You don't buy a poppy do y*ou?*   *You* don't see why *you* should!

You don't wear a poppy do *you?*   *You* don't see why *you* should!

You don't think what others gave
do *you?*   *You* don't see why *you* should!

You don't remember do *you?*   *You* don't see why *you* should!

You don't hear the cries of the
wounded do *you?*   *You* don't see why *you* should!

You don't fear the night do *you?*   *You* don't see why *you* should!

You don't feel in their debt do *you?* *You* don't see why *you* should!

You don't understand that do *you?* *You* don't see why *you* should!

You don't give a damn do *you?*   *You* don't see why *you* should!

You don't buy a poppy do *you?*   *You* don't see why *you* should!

BUT I CANNOT NAME THEM ALL

*(During the War, we met many new friends. We called them 'mate'
sometimes, but they were much more important than just a mate. They
were comrades, something very special to us, for we knew that if in
need and it was possible, help was always there.)*

I remember them,
They do not age,
They are the same, but I cannot name them all.

But I can see every wrinkle on their face,
Their little smile that meant so much,
They are the same, but I cannot name them all.

The laugh that showed such joy,
The 'good luck mate', that meant so much,
They are the same, but I cannot name them all.

Their cheery joke,
Perhaps the last that we might enjoy,
They are the same, but I cannot name them all.

It meant so much when out of luck,
And thoughts of death or something worse,
They are the same, but I cannot name them all.

We'd seen it all, you see before. The mine, the bomb, the burst of fire,
That changed us from our usual mould, and stopped
so many growing old.
They are the same, but I cannot name them all.

THE PADRE CAME TO SEE ME; HE HELD MY HAND IN PRAYER, AS HE KNELT BESIDE MY BED.

The Padre came to see me, with a cheery voice, and asked,
'How are you today 'My Son',
And getting on and coping,
With the problems that you have'?
'I also want to make sure, and certain,
That you are not feeling guilty at being here,
While your friends and comrades, are still fighting, over there,'
He said, 'I know it's tough for you lying in a cosy bed,
With the knowledge, that your friends and comrades
Are fighting still,
And so many others, are dead,'
'But 'My Son' there is a reason,
That you must understand,
That maybe you've been picked
Perhaps, for a special job for you to do.'
'Don't come it', I thought 'Padre',
But I didn't say a word,
But thought about the puzzle,
And wondered what he meant,
For as far as I had thought, till then,
I was there, for my time had come,
In fact, was overdue,
And nothing else was meant,
'I ask you 'My Son','
He said, in a special tone,
'You must take a special interest in
What there will be, for you to do
To make certain that you and your Comrades
And what you've all been through
Will make sure that after this is over
It was not a waste,
And all that you have suffered
(For that would bring, disgrace),

So, in the future, you
And your Comrades, must understand
The importance of your place,
In the coming scheme of things,
And do the very best you can
To take and act in a very special way,
And in full measure, too
In the task allotted you
In the saving the World from the ruin,
That is taking place
And you must make it certain
That when 'The Peace' is won,
At a cost that you and your Comrades are aware
That *the peace is not lost again*
By Man's inhumanity to Man.'

IN CRISPY SHEETS WE LAY!

(There can be no greater contrast than the battlefield with its filth, terror and insecurity and the cleanliness, kindness and security of a Military Hospital well away from the Front. But even then, it is not all peace as one lays between the crispy sheets with thoughts and sympathy for one's comrades still at the Front, who still need our thoughts and prayers.)

In crispy sheets we lay,
Caring not if night or day,
Tended by a kindly nurse,
When everything was worse.
Our thoughts were far away
With our comrades left behind,
In the dirt and grime,
And the terror of it all,
While in crispy sheets we lay.

Flavia Jarrett

I have been writing poetry since the tender age of eleven. I am now eighteen years of age and I must say I do feel extremely proud to see how my writing has gone from strength to strength. I live and grew up in inner city Birmingham. I find that the inner city lifestyle has as many advantages as disadvantages and really you must try to gain the best possible from an environment. Overall I believe I have enjoyed my time in Birmingham. I have encountered many interesting and meaningful situations that have given me the maturity to stay focused and to remain open minded no matter what the issue.

If you take a look at my writing you may notice that many of my poems either uncover a part of my life or segments of my thoughts. Each poem although sometimes may refer to an emotionally unhappy event, always I try for an element of hope. The poems I have submitted for this anthology are similar to me as an emotional index of mainly feeling and memories.

I write poetry mainly to relieve my pain and anguish. I feel that for me this is the safest method of therapy. My main influence would have to be my family breakdown and the mental confusion I suffered through this, although I do feel from this negative I have generated a positive output the can be accepted by myself and hopefully beneficial to the many that will read it.

If I was a doctor I think I would prescribe creative writing as penicillin for emotional bacteria! It has no serious side effects, no hangover and although the problem still may not have gone, it is definitely shared and lightened.

On a note to conclude this passage, I dearly hope my work reaches people that either understand or have been in similar situations. I would also like to think that hopefully some young person out there will read my work and even be influenced to write themselves because it really does help! I would also like to take the opportunity to thank Denise, Aubrey and Jahan.

POETRY

A talent that performs
And creates an image,
The image of a story . . .
That you have to unwind,
Like the secrets of a women
Like a script written . . .
With the power of the mind.

LOVE OR OBSESSION

Nothing could be colder than a breath upon your shoulder
A whisper of true loves due
But when this whisper turns to shouting on each and every outing
It's now time to find someone new

Let the key of desire enter into fire
Let your mind be spiritually free
Take a token of devotion
But not release the potion . . .

Because some things are not meant to be!

Trust your intuition,
Give good recognition for help that has been given
Do not take too lightly to treatment that's unkindly
A nature which does not suit you.

THE OPTIMIST

The optimist will always optimise
And make out the best from the worse
The optimist will always see a wish . . .
In each and every curse.

THE REAL HORROR IS LIFE

Watching a horror does not scare
Because I know when it's finished, it's finished!
On the other hand reality, I dare not to care,
As reality, no bounds nor limits.

Issues arise of poverty and greed
Passionate but deadly wars,
People in Africa planting a seed . . .
A seed that should fight for a cause!

Floods of ash
And volcanic teardrops,
Has this world gone ballistic?
Kill to make peace?
War to solve issues?
I really don't understand this

We've got it all wrong . . .
We must make it right!
How can you make peace . . .?
If you can't see the light.

The real horror is life!

OUR WORLD

Our world just keeps turning around and around
One day it's tranquil,
One day it's strife,
Sometimes the husband,
Sometimes the wife.

Some days I love it
Some days I don't
Some days I get it,
Some days I won't.

Who holds the power that's what I ask?
For the person who holds it hasn't half got a task!

Our world is mysterious
Our world is on fire,
'It's a game' people say.
But who's the umpire?

Who makes it rain?
Who invented snow?
Why we have feelings . . .
I may never know?

But from this poem I hope to achieve and believe . . .
That this world where we live is a valuable place . . .
That is here for all of us, wealth, creed and race.

FEELINGS

If a colour was a feeling,
Then a rainbow I would be,
Mixed emotions,
Funny feelings,
Swirling around in me.

If a cloud was a problem,
Then a cloud I would be,
Getting people angry,
Them shouting at me.

If the ocean was a bath,
That's where I would be,
Swimming all alone,
Perfect tranquillity.

If the sun was a key,
I would open up my heart,
Think of what I want,
And set a fresh start.

If my body was a clock,
I would set myself each day
Making sure I face a problem,
And do not run away!

Sometimes I just think . . .
Everyone makes mistakes,
When in trouble just remember . . .
Life gives but also takes.

BIRTHDAYS
(A poem written for Graeme Moore)

Your birthday is a special day
As this is the day of your birth,
And as well as you I value this day
It is the day you were placed on this earth.

Your birthday is a gift to me
Something we can share,
As a date in our new history,
And a memory that is rare.

A wish for all the joy and fun
In every kind of way
For you my dear and special one, who's birthday is today!

POETRY IS AN ART!

The stress of death,
Life is a test,
Poetry is an art.

The pain of power,
Our life hereafter,
I don't know where to start.

A solemn prayer,
A dangerous dare,
Like poison in a dart.

A promised secret,
A man of cheap wit,
A woman called a tart.

Sarcastic behaviour,
Jesus Our Saviour,
Mysteries lie in the heart.

Deep mystic charm,
Tranquil and calm,
This, the interesting part.

Why we hate love
And why we love hate,
These two are never apart.

The stress of death,
Life is a test,
Poetry is an art!

SIMPLY THE BEST

Simply the best
Simply desirable.
Simply the best
Something reliable.

A friend or a relative
Whom you hold trust,
A love that is love, rather than lust!

A tear that is true
A secret shared,
The respect of one's view
An opinion aired

A message of peace
So no more war,
Promise kept,
To abide our law.

A sense of intuition
A sense of belief
A guided tuition
To learn all we need.

Simply the best
And simply unique,
Life is our test,
That tests our belief!

FAITH

Faith is a word which I find hard to explain,
Faith in God, power or fame,
Faith is the link between me and you
If your faith helps you grow
Your faith must be true.

Faith, an element combined with hope,
Without my faith,
I couldn't cope!
Faith can triumph
Faith is belief
Valued and precious
Like a golden wreath.

Faith is the source that will see you through,
If your faith helps you grow
Your faith must be true!

IF I ONLY HAD A FATHER!

If I only had a father . . .
Someone I could trust,
The only man who'd look at me . . .
With pure love and no lust.

Someone to look out for me
Someone who would guide
Someone there to discipline
But also to confide.

A man whom I respected
To always feel secure,
Feeling safe and protected
His presence being my cure

A father who would tell me
'Your boyfriends are not right.'
He'd even sit and think of me . . .
When I'm asleep at night.

He'd know me inside out
And read me like a book,
He'd know when I was lying . . .
He'd know just by my look!

Someone I would care for
Someone who'd be true,
A person I would trust . . .
To debate my point of view.

Full of ambition
Helping to direct,
What to be his mission?

To love and protect.

                    If I only had a father
                    I would truly know . . .
                    If all I have just written
                    Was good or bad you know?

UNIQUE FRIENDS

Have you ever questioned a friendship?
Do you ever think out aloud?
Do you ever feel real neglected?
Does this friendship make you feel proud?

Is your heart full of sorrow?
Does this friendship keep you strong?
Do you secretly think of tomorrow?
Or is tomorrow too far and long!

Friendship should be like a flower
Each petal blows in the wind,
A bud that separates slowly . . .
And a centre that's so tight, it clings

A friendship can last a lifetime
Or it may only last a day!
The key to a long time friendship . . .
Is stay true, try hard, and pray.

HER THOUGHTS . . .

Thoughts of anger
Thoughts of hate
Thoughts of life,
And some mistakes.

Thoughts of laughter
Many jokes
Thoughts and memories,
And then provokes . . .

To tell a tale of love or lust
A red red rose turns into rust!

A jewel so bright
An eye so true,
Arises a pathetic view.

The summer radiant
The winter cold
A friendship aged,
A soul that's sold.

When trust is broken
Hearts are true,
When I realise change
New company too!

Jean Tyler

I spent my first quarter of a century in Liverpool where I was born and attended Medical School, and I enjoy that city's poets. I have lived in Devon for over forty years where my late husband was a Veterinary Surgeon. I am a retired GP with time-consuming interests in community projects, local drama and operatic groups, organ playing and choral music, gardening and my small flock of Devon Longwool sheep.

I have always 'scribbled' poetry and prose for my own amusement, but since joining a writers' group a few years ago, have taken this addiction more seriously. Committing thoughts and anxieties to paper especially in times of crisis, has been therapeutic: initially the emotions seem to settle more comfortably on the page than in conversation. In lighter vein I find it easier to idly criticise or poke fun at colleagues or local situations in some rhyming nonsense than in stark spoken appraisal!

The opportunity to listen to others' work at 'First Thursday', my writers' group has added another dimension to my interest and it was their sporadic approval which encouraged me to submit pieces which have appeared in Poetry Now, Triumph House, Arrival Press and Anchor Books publications. So here I am, submitting a whole lot more, which has been a good exercise in itself!

SURVIVAL OF THE SPECIES

He came keenly at three with ostensibly a mission
To revise and teach her more about binary fission
She warmed to his subject, human biology
An essential ingredient for the June GCSE

They studied inflorescence of the plantain and the thistle
The calyx and corolla, the carpels and the pistil
Then moved onto the earthworm and its adult reproduction
On the surface of the lawn, a nocturnal seduction

Thence to crawling crayfish which mate late in September
And cockroaches which turn their backs to make love and remember
They continued through the gamut of Darwin's evolution
The dogfish and the frog with its well-known spawn solution

And finally to mammals where they made a close connection
Understood so well the natural selection
They made love on a Sunday in the heat of afternoon
Both fresh and nubile virgins, he came a sperm too soon

Years later tho' in harness with a splendid A N Other
She still knows deep nostalgia for her first, her student lover
A wormcast on the grass, a frogspawn distribution
Make her smile quietly for - Darwin's evolution

A LIFE INSIDE

How long was his life?
As long as we remember
Accomplished in the warm
Of a womb one soft September

First movements brought great joy
Enhanced anticipation
Then disturbed with super strength
A drowning desperation

He was born completely still
A stillbirth to the world
Body beautiful complete
A wisp of hair that curled

He saw none of the people
Very few saw him
And yet we hurt with loss
Grief flowing from the brim

In mind he'll live for ever
In the brightness of the dawn
A glowing evening sunset
A lamb just newly born

A swallow may fly early
Leave the milling flock
Mount a soaring thermal
Leave a life in hock

No-one is ever lost
Intangible an essence
Lingers gently on
A comfortable presence

DARWIN'S BABY

I'm waiting for a baby, not mine, but for my daughter
At forty, this her third, she wants it under water
I know that it's quite fashionable to do it now like this
But is it really natural to give birth like a fish?

Then I think of evolution - we pass through Pisces on the way
With a phase of nearly gills early in the day
Of the months of embryology when the babe is on the way.

So I suppose . . .
To the underwater genera we are sort of related
Darwin's tale of evolution must not be underrated
Then again the baby's carried in an ante-natal fluid
In fronded folds of membrane, draped like an ancient Druid.

When a birth is started by a trigger quite miraculous
And the boy or girl is born and steadily looks back at us
It breathes the air and cries and everyone's exalted
But if it is submerged, the response is briefly halted
Until it softly surfaces, then plucked from naissance water
Gives reassuring signs of life. This is Genevieve, a daughter

And so it ended happily, tho' seventeen days late
At 10lbs the family's heaviest, that is so far to date
The cord was stretched to breaking just before the birth
And big sister Lily's news at school provided sweetest mirth

'My mum has had a baby,' (solemnly this is spoken)
'In a bath, I've got a sister, but the chain got broken.'

MORTAL LINKS

A generations outing, a brilliant day in March
Granny, elder daughter, daughter's daughter Lily Darch
They walk the quay at Hartland, spy a fulmar's nest
(Lily is just three years old and talks her very best)

They picnic in a field upon the family rug
And spread out all the goodies from the ancient family trug
Later they hike to Stoke, view the churchyard stones
And read historic glimpses of long-disjointed bones

Mother's fingers trace the letters, wind-smoothed and lichen-green
Dispel the granite's fetters to read who may have been
Head, foot and body stones with heavy load beneath
Of fatal births and fevers and shipwreck-stricken grief

Her voice is low, respectful with eternal fascination
Which attends the ends of others' lives, their final destination
She and Granny quietly muse upon the graveyard scene
Forget just for a moment their charge, the Lily queen

They hear a plainsong voice, see her touch a stone
And make out she is reading as her mother's done
'I'm sorry you are dead and cannot see your friends
But when you're bad you all get killed and that is how it ends!'

Amazed they gazed at Lily
Stunned to silence, well almost
'Holy Mother' Granny said
Lily's mother, 'Holy Ghost!'

FLEETING PHILOSOPHY

'Lily does not listen in the class,'
Such alliteration lined her school report
She was lively, five, going on fifteen
But showed no interest in being taught

Her mother was quite sad and disappointed
Asked her daughter why this should have been
And waited quietly for an explanation
From the Daddy's girl, the little Lily queen

Lily frowned and wrinkled up her nose
Full-faced with puzzlement and strife
'On listening, I'm not that keen, in face I've really never been
I need the time to get on with my life.'

NIRVANA

Pills and pillows
Restless billows
Wills and will-o'-the-wisp
Strips and stains
Drips and drains
Whiteness done to a crisp

Cleanliness
Light-headedness
Copious analgesia
Distant pain
Felt again
After anaesthesia

Life in limbo
Arms akimbo
Limp dependant tubes
Artificial
Sacrificial
Unsupported boobs

I must wait
In this state
Entering the world
Trust my carers
Health repairers
Till my brain's unfurled

FRESH AIR

Each spring is better than the last
And takes me by surprise
When a soft wind blows its promise
Through pale blue cottoned skies
And shimmers blackthorn's leaf-bared blossom
Shafts primrose yellow light
Whispers dainty daffodils
To launch a Brimstone flight

It stirs the long-grown winter lawns
And trees poised with buds on hold
Starlings waiting for their mating
Till sun warms grey to gold

In the long drear of short winter days
When Christmas and family have been
I fear the mind's dark cloud may never lift
To let the spring come in
But the threshold of this changing season
Brings sharp anticipation
Of colour, light, revival
Re-birth, a new gestation

And each faithful spring is better than the last
And tho' I love the summer and the fall
I am truly convinced, today anyway
That my last spring will be the best of all

WINDOW-GLAZING

I'm sitting at the window
There's not a lot to see
The Fletcher's phlox is dying
And they're out at 33

Oh but goodness, here's Miranda
With the newest baby boy
In a Royal Marine blue pram
Spick, span, and ship ahoy

She looks prim, pert and cocky
Turns her head to preen
Achieving life's endeavour
At just turned sweet sixteen

She smiles at Ted the milkman
As he struggles with the key
(He's put old Winnie's milk inside
Since nineteen ninety three)

The dustman's due today
Maggie moved the sacks
To the gate-less grey stone entrance
Full of gaping cracks

I hope they come to time
Before the meals on wheels
Balanced by big Brenda
In her clip clop, tip top heels

Tomorrow will be Saturday
Sometimes the family calls
With all their questions -
'Have you had one of your falls?'

Well actually, I have
But to tell would be my doom
I mean to stay and live my way
Here in my own front room

RECURRING THEME

This summer has been wet, more like a monsoon
Few garden teas or barbecues, so autumn comes too soon
The bog needs little doing, that garden's flourished well
All big-leaved wet and shady where Tawnies screech and yell
And this year's frogs have flopped about - happily they shimmer
In filtered light and so avoid my overactive strimmer

Oh yes, it's 'mists and mellow fruitfulness', but there's end of
season clearing
Before the nights are all drawn in and thick frosts have a hearing
Which will sweeten all the parsnips: the peas and beans are finished
The cabbage white has made quite sure the sprouts will be diminished
Most of the lettuce bolted while I was away
But the onions are quite splendid and will last for many a day

The courgettes were delicious picked when young and narrow
Yet every year there's one I miss until it's made a marrow
Beetroots are on the small side but well-rounded dark and neat
The peppers smooth and green, unconscionably sweet
I've emptied all the greenhouse, dug plants up with verve
Picked tail end green tomatoes for ritual preserve

I've rooted all the cuttings of fuchsia and hydrangea
Hibiscus and geranium and one odd un-named stranger
Six purple aubergines on a single stalk
Firm slender cucumbers, good with pickled pork
The potatoes a disaster punished by the blight
Next year I'll move them on and use a virgin site

Every year's the same but different and fresh
With the flowering and the fruitfulness from tended early crèche
Some say 'Oh all that work - refurbishing the pots
For ever cutting lawns, extending parsnip plots
You should move to somewhere smaller now you're not so young'
But I love this life's structure, I'll stay and dig the dung

MOONSHINE

Silver shafts of light
Palest of full moons tonight
Shifting through the trees

Shimmers dance a tune
Halting suddenly too soon
As clouds ride the breeze

A dark interlude
Hunters quietly rest and brood
Their prey take their ease

Moonlight wins a glare
Lightens up a foxes' lair
The scavengers' lees

Moons will wax and wane
New to full then new again
Circling through the years

Eleanor Millar Scott

I am 53 years old, married to Tony with two grown up daughters, Linda and Sharee. I am a busy wife and mum. I also take care of my 92 year old mum. I have been writing prose for the last eighteen years. I do not belong to any writer's groups, I am inspired by life in general. I write funny poems, Christian poems and sad poems. The saddest poem I have ever written was 'Death' it speaks of my feelings when I lost my brother Jim in a motorcycle accident in the Isle of Man in August 1984. Writing is a special gift so it's an extra bonus to share it with others. They are my inner thoughts and feelings, through them I hope to touch someone and give them hope, encouragement and a smile.

In January 1997 I was one of ten finalists in the UK in a competition run by Avon and OK magazine. I penned 'Don't Be Afraid' and enjoyed a wonderful trip to London.

I have had a few of my poems read on local radio and have read a selection at church groups.

My other interests are gardening and the countryside. I enjoy long walks in our beautiful forests with my family and our miniature Schnauzer Max.

I hope you enjoy reading my poems and are challenged by them. Thank you for taking the time to read them.

FEELINGS

Birds singing sweetly on a lovely spring day
The smell of a rose or new mown hay,
An unexpected parcel that the postman brings,
These are a few of my favourite things.

Bullets and bombs that only bring grief,
Robberies and stealing the works of a thief.
A home with no mum or maybe no dad,
These are the things that make me sad.

Old lonely people, all on their own
A little stray dog, in need of a bone.
A friend I can trust my secrets to share,
These are the things that make me care.

Good health, good times for days to come,
Days full of laughter, joy and fun.
May each of these things all come true,
For these are the things, I wish for you.

MATTHEW'S PRAYER

God bless my home, with mum and dad
Give them patience, when I am bad.
I'm only small, so I must explore,
The great big world is my open door.

Forgive my temper when I get cross,
Teach me to know, I can't be boss.
I like to win and have my own way,
I'm sorry Lord, when I disobey.

I try so hard to be real good,
I try to do the things I should.
I love my parents, they're so good to me,
An obedient child I'll try to be.

Lord hear and answer my little prayer,
Keep mum and dad in your loving care.
I know I've brought them lots of joy,
Even though, I'm a naughty boy.

Don't Be Afraid

When all around is dark and dim,
When you feel alone and sad within.
When all hope is gone and you're in despair,
Reach out, take my hand, for you I'll care.

Don't be afraid, let me be your friend,
My trust and my time to you I'll lend.
Just like you, I've know pain and sorrow,
Worried and wondered, can I face tomorrow.

But just like a storm that passes with time,
Life's dark clouds are changed to sunshine.
Our burdens are lightened by a word or smile,
A touch, that tells us today was worthwhile.

So don't give up, for you're never alone,
Let me inspire you with the words of my poem.
Let me remember you each day in prayer,
Linked by a love chain, let me be there.

DADDY'S GIRL

I recall those happy days when I was Daddy's girl
When he would bounce me on his knee and set my heart awhirl.
Gee up Neddy, he'd sing to me as I listened to him there.
Upon my daddy's knee, I never had a care.

Swiftly the time has rolled along and left me a treasure chest,
Filled with precious memories, the sweetest and the best.
When days are dark and dreary, or I feel alone or sad,
I open up my treasure chest, given by a loving Dad.

I see my daddy's smiling face, I see his dancing eyes,
Sparkling brighter than twinkling stars, more blue than summer skies.
I see his arms outstretched to me, waiting to hold me tight,
Gently around me, they'd secretly fold, just like a blanket
on a cold wintry night.

I hear his voice, the voice I love, I hear him call for me,
I'd claim a thousand welcomes when I'd run to Daddy's knee.
What fun we'd share together he was my special friend,
He gave enough love to last me, until my journey's end.

Thank you for my treasure chest, for all that has been mine,
Thank you for your kindness, your patience and your time.
Those happy days will never fade, my heart is still awhirl,
No need for words, I know it's true, I'm still my daddy's girl.

MOTHER

Her face may be wrinkled, her hair has turned grey,
To me she grows sweeter with every new day.
Her step's much slower, than it used to be,
But Mother, I tell you, you're still precious to me.

Yes through the years these changes take place,
But no one can take the smile from your face.
Or no one can change your love and care,
Or the special times together we share.

So when I count my blessings, which God has given me,
I thank him for these special things, that I alone can see.
I thank him for your care, your kindness and your time,
But Mother, most of all I'm thankful, you are mine.

MY FARMER FRIEND

I met my gentleman farmer, many years ago,
Listen as I tell what Noel was like to know.
He walked along life's highway, in a very relaxing way
A calmness he gave to others, he met from day to day.

I admired his love for his land and home,
Content in this place, he'd no need to roam.
His friendly ways soon stole my heart,
In his life and home, I became a part.

The door of his home was always open wide,
He'd make you very welcome, once you stepped inside,
There he would be with his feet at the stove.
Having a wee quiet nap.
The kettle would be boiling for a cuppa, followed
By a good ole chat.

It's now been over thirty years, since I met my farmer man,
My feelings for him are still the same as when they first began,
I was proud to say, he's a friend of mine,
He became more precious with the passing of time.

He was someone you could trust, someone kind and true,
Someone loved by everyone, men like him are few.
Alas! Early one Sunday morning, death stole
My friend away.
This heart that grew to love him now, had a price to pay.

My face was washed with my flowing tears
For the friend loved and lost at seventy years.
I couldn't bear to see him in a coffin cold and still
No voice, no smile, no one his place can fill.

So thank you Lord for the times we shared,
For the memories he's left, the way he cared,
I pray he's with you, just having his nap.
And one day I'll join him, and we'll have a good chat.

MY HOMELAND

Beautiful homeland of Ireland, the place I love so well,
Amidst your glorious splendour, I'm content and happy to dwell.
No artist could paint your picture or poets write in rhyme,
No singer could capture the melody sealed in this heart of mine.

My Emerald Isle, with its forty shades of green,
Sleepy little leafy glades with babbling dancing brooks between.
The loftiness of mountains, the billows from your sea,
Land of myth and magic, you mean so much to me.

But mingled with your sweetness, I see your hurt and pain,
I see the scars that marred you, as I hang my head in shame.
I've heard the bombs that ravaged and torn us all apart,
I've seen the weeping mother, with deep sorrow in her heart.

As the advent of the millennium dawns upon our land,
Embrace each other with friendship, reach out a helping hand.
Heal the pain and suffering, bathe it with your love,
Can't you hear the pleading? Our land has had enough.

A 50s LAMENT

Today is very special Dawn, so why do you look so sad?
Celebrating your big 50th, isn't really that bad.
But maybe I should warn you of what now lies in store,
Then it won't be so scary, even though I'll sound a bore.

It's a funny time of life, you're kind of in-between,
You're neither young or neither old, middle-aged is what I mean.
You're too old to boogie, yet too young for the pensioners' club,
You feel you're like a worn out car, nothing but a dud.

Remember I speak from experience, so listen to all I say,
Just heed my words of wisdom, and you'll chase your blues away.
Smile when you find another grey hair, don't just grump and sigh,
Accept it's a sign of ageing, go out and buy a dye.

Don't wear your specs when you look in the glass,
The wrinkles seem less and you think, ain't I first-class.
When you say, that's right when you know you're wrong,
It's not the wax, it's your hearing that's gone.

It's now size twenty instead of ten, diets are a thing of the past,
Too late for aerobics or even jogging, the ole ticker would never last.
Thick elastic stockings you'll wear on your legs to hide your
                                            varicose veins.
A massage with deep heat will be a thrill, it'll ease your
                                            rheumatic pains.

Accept my birthday greetings Dawn, they come with all my love,
I'll be here to give advice whenever your days are rough.
Don't fight the battle all on your own, it's hard to stay alive,
Just think on me, then tell yourself, I know I will survive.

BABY

Little baby small and sweet,
With tiny hands and tiny feet.
I watch you as you're sleeping there,
Content and happy, without a care.

Mother kind has you tucked up tight,
In a lovely blanket with colours bright.
To keep you cosy, to keep you warm,
Here in your pram where nothing can harm.

Love and care is all you need,
Every four hours you look for a feed.
A nappy clean to keep you dry,
Give you these and you seldom cry.

For days ahead I wish you health,
A precious gift, much better than wealth.
May God bless you each new day,
As you grow in his wisdom and follow his way.

SNOW

So quietly you come, without a sound,
Lightly and gently you cover the ground.
There you lie so clean and bright,
Brightening up this winter night.

Why do you come and cover the land?
Why do I hold you so tight in my hand?
Why do you make me love you so?
Why do I sigh when I see you go?

I watch the children having such fun,
Playing with you in this winter sun.
Then very soon, what's this I see,
It's you friend, snowman looking at me.

I wish you could stay for a week, or more,
But the rain doesn't like you, so down he pours.
Away you go without saying goodbye,
This is the reason you make me sigh.

I'M JUST ME

I'm eleven years old and I want to have fun,
I never listen to my dad or mum.
They always tell me how I should be,
But I disobey, 'cause I'm just me.

Stay away from the river, don't go up the town,
Stop climbing trees you naughty boy, in case you tumble down.
Stop kicking that old football, it's time you had your tea,
I pretend I never heard, 'cause I'm just me.

Play with your little sister, tidy up those toys,
You're not going swimming with those other rowdy boys.
Get your homework finished, you can't watch TV,
I turn away and mutter, 'cause I'm just me.

Don't do this, don't do that, is all I hear each day,
I know I shouldn't be naughty and want to have my way.
I'm sorry I don't listen, an obedient boy I'll be,
So please forgive me Mum and Dad, 'cause I'm just me.

Heather Tweedie

I was born in Ulster in 1934. My mother was an orphan of Scots origin who came to live in N Ireland where she met and married my father. He was one of nature's gentlemen and a frustrated academic. He had a great love of classical English literature which he instilled in me by encouraging me to read. I had a reasonably happy childhood and in 1952 I went to London to study speech and language therapy and here I became introduced to modern poetry.

I married in 1956 and with my husband and four children went to a seaside village where I developed my first love of the sea and moorland. My first poem was written here and I have continued to write - not on command - I cannot write rhyming poetry as I cannot express my thoughts in that form.

I often rise with the dawn and write a poem triggered off by an incident from the previous day. I am 'a born actress' quote tutor at RADA but was not permitted to 'go on the stage'.

I was lucky to find world books and some small publicity outlet for my work. My sincere wish is to be a good writer and to write according to the dictates of my personal emotional life influenced by my past.

I have written a day diary since 1969 which forms the basis of a book - who knows?

A Girl And Her Field

She placed her hands and her bare feet
On the sun-hot metal of the barred gate.
She let herself down into the summer field,
The fray topped purple grass was silky to touch;
Tentatively she walked alone chewing a blade of grass,
Feeling the dry lumpy earth between her toes.
A herd of bullocks trampled out a path approaching her,
A fraction of fright touched her heart;
She stood very still while the soft wind blew her hair
Across her eyes and lips:-
The bullocks halted. Waited.
Bent their pendulous necks to resume their steady grazing
Ignoring the intruding stranger.
The sun's rays faded; a chill went through her body,
The girl turned her face away and with reluctant steps
She left her cooling field.

MONSOON RAIN

A Jacob's ladder of lightning angled up to the moonless sky
An orchestral cacophony of tympani thundered to a climax
At the crest the drums rolled softly away to a dark rhythmic beat.
The dissonant sound of unrelenting rain beat the heavy banana leaves,
The coconut palms swayed slightly in the windless humidity;
Warm and wet the luscious blossoms raised up their faces to the torrent
Sometime a defeated petal falling to the sodden earth.
Sharp elongated pine rods of rain drove out the frogs trumpeting in
                                        an agony of delight,
The human mind restlessly begging for relief from the imprisonment
                                                of the noise
Powerless before this terrible force of nature's uncompromising
                                        punishment.

AGE

The punk green grows in the spring
At the root of the tree
Until the motor of maturity cuts its spikes into convention,
Only to come again
And flourish on the sap of the earth,
To live the vital years and procreate in the spanning of life
Consumed by its tenuous emotions.
The sun at its ultimate height
Dries it brown, until it fades and dies
Leaving a space and flake encrusted scalp,
Inevitably to dwindle out the years of its final span.

A STORM

God's thunder is in the torrid sea
Spume cracks on the treacherous eternal rocks.
Long evil breakers rise and fall on impact stirring the whirlpool foam.
No gentleness at the water's edge
Only sludge sand raised from the ocean bed.
The soul of the ocean howls the song of the falling darkness,
The whipping wind that leaves no breath
Churns up the grey retracted light.
Knowledge of fear stirs in the currents of the heart,
Eddies of madness and gross insanity
Boil beneath the surface of the schizophrenic sea.

A THAILAND HOLIDAY

Diamonds, not fake, brilliantly cut the still water
Slivering in glances of light
The idle rich slide their oily bodies into this turquoise pool
Emerge to order wine from those who clasp the hands and bow
Dignified in their primitive lives of poverty.
Proud and contained they live with the odour of sewage,
Content with their Buddha creed of holy need, not want,
They consume the sun respendently beating on their golden bodies
Sheening their black silk oriental hair,
They force on us humility as we briefly share their land,
Soon to return to the cold rat race of common humanity.

A ROUGH SEA CRUISE

The woman's red burnt body sings and stings
In the howling and moaning of banshee summer wind,
Crazily she rides the waters in the name of pleasure
Watching the gallery rail dip and fall on the horizon.
The phosphorescence of the waves becomes a dissolution;
Where is the moon on this other side of the world.
At night she gives her body up to the heavy swell.
Doors are locked and danger signs are posted against the wind.
What punishment is being meted out to her
On this far off Caribbean Sea,
Peace she knows would come if she reached the rock hard ocean bed,
She strains for the familiar steadiness of home.

AN INDUCED ABORTION

Empty vacated womb
A male child born in the dawn chorus
A deformed memory
His ashes scattered nowhere.
Hot, weak her soiled body
Tortured by untutored hands
Makes the cries quiet now
Unable to express the unexpected death.
They did not comprehend her numbness,
Nor the grief hidden in the dark corners of her mind.
Where was the grief that she should feel?
It would come in later years to drive her out of her mind
Another kind of pain.

A Night In A Bowel Ward

Put the blanket over your head
Cut out the desperate sounding agony of regurgitated faeces.
Try to ignore the pain
Slashing through your bowel.
Look at the dimmed balls of light above
In the darkness of the ward.
Hear an ancient voice tremulously call 'Nurse, nurse.'
You pray for sleep to bring oblivion
From the vile smells, the padding feet,
The clattering bed pan, caused by those who care
                        for us in this hideous sanctum.

THE VIOLET

Stooping at the hedgerow
She touched the trembling stem
The delicate head drooped
Strength in its utter innocence.
Fragile silken petals of the violet
Throbbing with the sap of life;
To pluck it is to commit an act of murder
Crushing it as her young virginity.
Bitterly she snapped the stem.
Stroked the fluttering petals as he had stroked
                                   her silken body.
The precious flower was broken,
Dead as her lover whose ashes lie deep in the earth
The roots of love broken as the heart of the violet.

HOSPITAL

The patient's eyes were black in the globe filled nocturnal darkness,
Rest would not come to her painful irritated bowel.
Those who were caring did not smile in the sick night
But offered gentle words of practised comfort.
The noise of unfamiliarity - the clash of metal bed sides.
Broken tears from those who lost someone
Leaving disconnected tubes, a twisted sheet,
A man, a woman left, will sort the detritus mature beyond their years.
A bed is filled, a bed is emptied
In the classless society of the ill - the cured, the dead, the dying,
Sickness in its indignity is the leveller of all in every bacterial darkness.

WALKING THE BEACH

She meets a man
A native of this blessed place.
His sea bright eyes seek hers
And she feels the chemistry of their souls touch
As they pass each other; no innocent purpose.
She treads gently around the circles of the sandworms
Hidden from the oyster catchers
Who ignore her gentle presence
Running quickly, smoothly, urgently
On the gentle wind blown sands
Low to the earth in this place she has borrowed
For a snatch of her life time.

THE SOFT COUNTRY

The leaves enfold the wafting wind
And cradle it within their shivering boughs,
The hedges staunch resist its flow
With hip and haw and blackberry.
The delicate strength of the horse
Walking across the hoof mushed grass
To take the apple from my hand
With eager velvet lips and dirty yellow teeth,
Ears pricked he nuzzles my chest with harsh affection.
I, stroke the long head bone beneath his wind tangled mane,
Blow softly up the grey black nostrils.
No fumes, no tarmac, no sooty smell of town dried clothes.
The wellingtons tread the uneven field,
And when I return and walk the road
I'll see a blade of oil-streaked grass
And in my soul I will remember.

LOVE

To know is to want
To want is to love
To the infinite infinity to love.
As the soaring movement of a crashing wave
Crush me in the depth of your desire
Pull me to the whirlpool of the deep
Tangled with swaying weed,
Slimy and wet as my femininity,
Strong as the underflow of my love.
As the currents of the cruel sea
Violent in the ultimate strength comes a terrible stillness,
My body beats as continuous as the motions of the deep.

THE DEATH OF A LOVER

Fragile as parchment one petal falls
Brown and twisted round the edges
Craving the sun, the earth, the light.
Bitter she tramped on the unseen flower
The sap of its life ceased to flow,
The heartbeat stopped.
Another petal ground into the earth
So still at last in peace.
Withered, ashen and crumpled
Thus the life of her lover left his body
And her spirit knew its first maturity of grief.

A Sunny Morning

Tiny slivers of silver water
Caress the ribbed sand
Reflected from the streak of sunlight.
Penetrating the far dim mist of the shadowed mountain
Beyond the slow andante of the warm morning.
All alone in the pristine wrack smelling peace
She sits in perfect harmony with the sky,
No sighing of the wind or falling mist or rain
Only the crushed shell heat of sand
Bearing its burden of slimy shipwrecked wrack.

DEPRESSION

Sitting by the window wrapped in a blanket
Her handkerchief sodden
With the drowning rain of tears;
The sky as dark as the dead eyes of her depression
A voice in her mind calls out 'Seek me'
But there is no help for her, in the passage of time
Memories stir and unwillingly
The wave splash of tears flows down her cheek,
She must learn to live again
Learn to plunge her naked body
In the violent ocean of life.
There is no light at the end of the tunnel
Only Hell's promise of a sort of death.

Norman Royal

'A Darker Shade Of Sun'.

'I believe -
That before life
Was first formed
Out of an ocean,
It was born
From a tear.'

DREAM WITHIN A DREAM

Count the stars,
Each one
A pearly string
Of Dream,
Put to sleep
The angels
Of the evening,
Behind
The moonlight
Of your eyes.
Feel the spring
Breeze
Of a thousand
Wing flutters
As your beating
Heart within
Stays with me,
Until the mists
Of new morning
Touches the sun.

SHADOWRAIN

I watch you now
Through the shadow rains
Of your dream.

You sleep
In silver clouds
Of moonbeam's calling.

There is a tear
Upon your pillow,
Moist lashes
From a broken storm.

Where do you go to
When the night owl calls
And your room
Makes patterns
Of falling leaves
Around you?

You once believed
In unicorns
Peeping through
The forest glades,
Whilst I had
Only slain them.

SNOWFIRE

I will love you
Until
The moon
Is a jaggery brown
And the night lies resting
In sugar-sweet
Breathing of your dream
Like bowls of maple wine.
Until
The ice maidens of morning
Come gently whispering against
The windows of my soul
As the snow-fires
Of the stars go out
And this life
Is no longer mine.

A CASCADE OF STARS

Some nights
When the tangled moon
Moved on
Without you,
I would find
Your footprints
In the mirrors
Of stars.

Buttercup smiles
In
Autumn fires
Inviting,
Shy morning meadows
Of
Echoed Dream
To follow.

WHILST SHADOWS WATCH

She sleeps in
Crystal petals
Of peach dream,
With dewy tear
Held back
In weepy dark.

Her hair falls
Tousled
But untroubled,
Amongst the
Silver tresses
Of the pitched stars.

Moon flowing
Has stirred her
In the misty half light,
Her pillows are blushed
By the silk
Of moving planets.

Soon weightless hours
Are counted, awakened
In a timeless zone,
She will first touch
With love, the toiler
Of the earthly soil.
- Morning.

DARTMOOR PRISON (BENEATH YOUR MISTS)

Cold kissed dank mist
Completely blanket this blot.
Cover well this
Grey granite sight
Of Dartmoor's unsightly face,
So none may tell.

Hide for shame this house of numbers
Of countless men without a name.
Conceal their lack of hope,
Hopeless to reveal.
The truth at best be stifled
Suffocated under a vapoured air.

Chilly ghosts of a past forgotten
Who stone by stone built this icy tomb.
American and French prisoners of war
In their bondage of 1806.
It was a good year for the Empire,
Or so we all were told.

They built with bleeding hands acold
And clotted empty bellies raw.
Belay, they now where well fed dogs patrol
Within the sterile zone.
Bleached against a crumbling wall
Of mildew, moss and bone,
Yet still bonded to the system's control.

So seal tight you mists, don't lift
And of the ghosts whom haunt this place,
Leave them and I alone.

SPRING AWAKENS

Spring has awoken and stretches
With unfolding sleepy yawn,
Eyes half open, stirs and stumbles
Towards the sunlight's dewy lawn;
Toadstools' stubby heads to greet
With morning's promise of 'warmer'
And nods goodnight to winter, leaving
Crumbled pyjamas in their corner.

THE FRAGILE HEART

Hold my heart delicately
In your sweet cupped hands
Like an evening's shadow,
Feel its brief life flutters
Before you finally let it fall.

ELM AT HASLEMERE

Old man of the woods,
I see you now
Crawled naked
Beneath a slender frame.

You think to hold
Your blushes
Part showing
Such shy crinkled skin.

Tickling dry
Moist water moustaches,
A fringed smile hides
Surprise spring branches.

Karin said, 'Nearby
In summer uninterrupted,
Two grey squirrels
Tinged red would play.'

THE HUNGRY YEARS

Yes, I remember the days of peeling plaster
And I had seen clearly then
What lies beneath the skin.
No fancy front of make-believe,
Only the life that makes you thin.
As evening shadows fell so very young
Upon my empty bellied wall,
To dash the face of any illusion born,
Even before the dragging dream had any chance to form.

The rusty nail that hung the long night
Without the fancy frame,
As if the widening cracks of day
Were some deep meaning work of art, when they only
Meant the begging of deep chasms of dismay.
And the stalking moon would hide
Behind the agonising second hand
That strikes the empty hour.
Stopping me from painting what I really saw
When black hunger held the power.

And what's so good about the dream anyway?
When it lies cast off in the corner.
You can't wear it in the beating rain
When your shoes are letting in the water, and you are
Only walking back into dark pools of reality again.
And my mother was an angel in silent suffering
Who carried us safely across a chaotic sea
On just a steady believing thing.
And half an age on, I am still trying to attain
Some of her beauty that lay within.

RIVERS OF RED STONE

It's only the ripples in the sunset
Reflecting in the dark pools,
Like rich, ruby wine flows,
Shimmering over the still waters
To move the pebble stones,
Singing, 'Look how fast life goes!'

Just some moments in the main stream
Taking the time to pause,
Before the Afon Mynach leaps
Into the River Rheidol below,
And trying not to disturb in evening,
Where deep the dragon sleeps.

Some mirrored thoughts in the setting,
Touching now and then
Upon my island in the flowing;
Taking me to another time,
Sometimes oh! so slowly,
And sometimes without me even knowing.

But did you think that,
After all that has passed between us,
I would just let you sweep by today
Without a last tear, a fond farewell
To fall upon you,
To help you along your way?

ISLANDS

In his abstinence he has touched you much,
within that sterile zone of absence's dream.
The distance being the silent islands,
that yawns the wider sea between.
Becoming absorbent in his isolation
you drift undulant into your own;
and his island by its very nearness,
leaves you that much further alone.

You wonder the many reasons why,
becoming helpless in the stream.
Taken deeper into the mind's eye
answers, become the doubts there's been.
And you say, 'I thought so all along'
to yourself, but you are never really sure.
Your love is far more betrayed now
than of the love you had before;
and you surround yourself with hurt
against any tidal wave you can,
but in your distant island's view,
you just never asked the man.

REFLECTIONS FROM A DARK POOL

In the autumn of your years you would ask me,
Where has all your dark hair gone?
For now you are only finding
The wearing grey within;
And I would reply, 'That your silken hair,
Only holds the passing silver's reflection
From some running rivers nearby
In the moonlight, just to spin.'

And you would say, 'That it's getting much colder now
And that you can only see,
From within your dark eyes vision,
The misty evenings more.'
And I would reply, 'No! No! My love,
For looking far deeper within,
I can only see the warm blue
Just like, I always have before?

And you would say,
That the winter wraps around us
Like the sharp needled branches
From some old thorn tree, just to cling.
And I would reply, 'Well! Now is the time, my love
To reflect upon our young summers gone,
For can't you see along the stretching arms
The first budding shoots of spring?

Susan Serrano

Susan Serrano was born in Stoke-on-Trent, in the Midlands. She is a writer, artist, and lecturer in Spanish at Kingston University, Surrey. She has published books on poetry, philosophy, folklore, language and cuisine. Among these are: *A Treasury of Spanish Love Poems,* published in the USA as a book and also as an audio-book by Hippocrene Books Inc; *Spanish Proverbs, Idioms and Slang; A Spanish Family Cookbook; The Great British Teatime; The Vulgar Tongue: Oral Tradition in Spanish.* Her poems have appeared in many anthologies and journals in the UK, USA and Spain, including *Scintilla, Lexikon, New Hope, Poetry Inc, Translation Review* and *Equivalences.* Susan Serrano regularly exhibits her artwork, much of which is inspired by her poetry. She lives with her family in Surbition, Surrey.

Susan Serrano has described her latest poems as a 'labour of love to two cultures', and this is clearly reflected in some of the poems included here. With a bicultural sensibility, she paints a world where the colours, sounds, smells and images of England are melded with the courtyards, intimate interiors, history and myths of Southern Spain.

The poems evoke a poignant sense of place and time that reflect the author's powerful influences: from the convent-school upbringing, set against the backdrop of the industrial Midlands and the smut-disgorging chimneys in the Potteries, to the sensuous encounter with the sun-baked landscapes and vibrant culture of Andalusia. The section is a vivid mosaic of childhood memories, family and home, as well as the poet's encounter with the eternal themes of love, ambition, conflict, death, dream or reality - captured in the split lens of someone who lives between two contrasting worlds.

FIELDS OF VISION

We lived in those streets
they were our playground:
tag, rosy apple*, kerb-to-kerb tennis,
rounders and other unrestrained ball games -
with no thought for neighbours' windows
and no complaints either. Hopscotch towers
decorated the carless tarmac
awaiting our return from school
after tea.

In winter we'd make a slide:
compacting the snow along on a narrow strip
in the middle of the road
and bringing it to a hard shine
with our shoes
as we slithered down, over and over -
my turn next.
It glistened in the smoky-orange lamp-light
that smouldered on the murky air.
We made it. It was ours
and nobody could have a go on it
without our permission.
Hope it doesn't thaw tonight.

In summer, pinafored matrons
stood on doorsteps, looking on,
and the streets were our dominions
our fields of vision.

*Street game where children knock on neighbours' doors then run away

With a liquorice whirl
and sherbet dip
we sat on windowsills in the half light
or leaned against the wall
on the corner by the green painted lamp post
and talked about Elvis
till almost nine, waiting for the final call
that closed the door on silence
and our day.

67 TUNSTALL

At four o'clock we loped out of the convent gate -
aka Holy Joe's Primary, Wolstanton.
Hands digging in blazer pockets
we joined the scrum for a couple of ha'penny
blackjacks in the tuck shop opposite
then started the ascent to the bus stop.
Unchaperoned,
by the petrol station we'd wait,
a posse of nearly-eight-year-olds.
As soon as the 67 appeared on the crest
of the bend, arms aloft bopping the air
unrepressed
the chant went up: *67 Tunstall, 67 Tunstall . . .*
transparent smiles of pre-hygienist days
flashing jet-plated teeth and tongues.
Clambering aboard the top deck, we hauled
satchels bulging with long-division,
fractions, or spelling
                    and a l w a y s catechism.

The ten-minute ride took us down the hill
past the canal and the first podgy chimneys
disgorging smut (once we ran all the way there
to save a penny on the tuppenny fare,
pooling the coppers
we bought twelve multi-coloured
gobstoppers);
then on, skirting Brownhills, the grand Protestant grammar -
not a feature on our academic horizons -
until we reached The Square,
and a chorus of *see you tomorrows* sent us different ways.

My sister and I headed up through the town,
stopping outside The Ritz
to study the promotion stills for next week's film;
cutting through side streets, via the pot bank
where Granny worked daubing tea-pots with creamy slip,
we reached the avenue, and home -
in through the back-kitchen door
or window
            if we'd lost the key o n c e more.

First job: make the fire.
The house always seemed bare
and forsaken
with a dead hearth: *A fire's company,*
Auntie Rose used to say.
Newspaper, sticks, matches, coal
the drawing-pin (a great imperative hung
over the fire-making ritual: heart and soul)
a roaster-toaster was the required result,
and with it went a corresponding satisfaction
of a basic life-skill perfected.
Then some bread and jam, and homework
till teatime.
Kids today don't know they're born,
I can s t i l l hear
            Mrs Jackson mourn.

THE SUMMER WASH

It turned cold suddenly and early
this year, it seemed to me.
Summer ended on Friday 11th September
to be precise.
Now wistfulness engulfs
at the dying of the light
    chilly rooms
        torpor
and the thought of donning
ever more layers of apparel until . . .
perhaps early May.

Yes, I know autumn is a bewitching time
for poets: so much mellowness,
russets, olives and ochres, bountiful
apple trees, crackling log fires, inglenooks,
and allusions to the dappled-ripeness
of one's years. Halcyon days.

But I ache for the summer wash: cadmiums,
scarlets and aquamarine; the voluptuous
waft of a giddy ocean breeze
over a grateful body,
lingering Andalusian nights
that melt into ardent, palmy days
when the indolent sun,
high and mighty, lolls resplendent
as it ordains the earth with lustre
and manifests the full-bloom of life.

REFUGEE CONVOY

Refugee convoy
Bombed in error. Another
Cup of tea?

SWEET AND CLEAN

Her face was sweet,
her aspect clean,
just as she liked her washing
to smell: 'Peg it out and give it a blow,
duck, or it won't smell sweet and clean.'
'Yes, Gran.'
Shirts, vests, pants and all sorts
of that'll-come-in-useful cloths
hung on the line in her backyard,
propped between the coalshed
and the privy, prancing leadenly
in the sodden, smoky air
of that Potteries town.

Each time I scrape the last visible
traces of margarine from a tub,
leaving it waste-not clean,
I do it in sweet memory of you.

THE BRAZIER

Do you remember the long Andalusian evenings
whiled away in easy chat, gathered
around the skirted table of forever,
hands and legs snuggled beneath the warm
comforting cloth, when - before the safe, no-fuss
odourless heaters of today -
the mesmeric char of the brazier
rose to ruddy cheeks
and weave its slumberous spell?

Coals were arranged in that pan
as ceremoniously as gift offerings on any altar,
sprinkled with lavender and overlaid
with a canopy of mesh
as if in some sacred rite,
then, placed in its curtained tabernacle
within the inner sanctum
under the table,
the brazier was lit:

the secret of its bewitching embers
concealed beneath a venerable cloak.

BY THE POND

By the pond
the frogs sit motionless
S p l a s h!

EPICUREAN AROUSAL
(For Rafael)

There are few things
more pleasurable

than leisurely
engrossing
food

that indulges
hands
tantalizes smell
invites the eyes
caresses taste
and transports
the mind:

holding the palate suspended
in sensual anticipation
while

warm bread is broken
   a piquant salad dressed
      a mussel shell opened

and the voluptuous thought
that the seduction
has just
begun.

THE RACE

(Esse est percipi - To be is to be perceived: George Berkeley, Three Dialogues)

'Here he is again, look,'
said Will, passing the newspaper to his friend.
'Now he's written a book!
Bound to be read as a holy writ.
He's 28, t w e n t y e i g h t . . .
                                        jumped the gun,
oozing name and triumph,
on top of *le beau monde.*
There's no fathoming it,
some are just touched by that little magic wand
and there you have it, on a plate: life's winners.
Due payers like me, unrelenting, press on
sweat of the brow sinners
lose ground, condemned to falling in
with the troop of also-rans in the grand marathon.'

'At least you were in the race,' smiled the friend
'and made good time.
I was another 20 years up the hill
before I found the starting line
and I'm standing on it still
waiting for somebody to shout *Go!*
But start has turned into a finish sign.'

A DISTANT FIGURE

A distant figure
In the street I see your smile
Hasten towards me.

IRONING SHIRTS

'Another pile of ironing,' I croak,
dumping the crumpled shirts on the chair.
'Take it easy,' comes the mellow reply,
'you iron yours and I'll do mine.'

I know you want to help, to share,
I muse,
but doesn't such a rigid,
measured division of labour seem . . .
    mean of heart
      between two who love?

'No, I'll iron yours, and you iron mine,
then you'll be wrapped in my smoothing,
vaporous caresses all day long,
and I in yours.'

LOVE AND CHERISH

To be loved is blithe,
To be loved for what you are, blissful;
But to be cherished . . .
                         that is sublime.

To be cherished: held dear
to another's heart, treasured,
treated with tenderness,
                         what celestial felicity!

I am loved and cherished:
          I am blessed
            ennobled
               in a state of grace.
I am a God in my heaven.

EARLY-MORNING SLUMBER

In my warm bed
Through the dark
I listen to the wind and rain
Thrashing at the window
Tossing and turning
The storm rages on
As I close my eyes
Falling back into
Early-morning slumber
And recapture dreams
Still afloat.

Untitled

Sit down at the piano
In mid-November, standing
Up it is full spring.

Leslie Holgate

Les Cwmrod (pen name) born 20 April 1926, Hyde, Cheshire. Par Tom and :Lillian. Attended St Paul's Newton until aged 14 and night school and served an engineering apprenticeship at Daniel Adamson, Dukinfield, Cheshire.

I am a Registered Engineer and a retired member of two Professional Engineering Institutions. Served in World War II in the British Army units in the Middle East and with the British Merchant Navy as Engineer Officer. Met my wife Jean Almond in 1948 and married in 1951, and will be celebrating a Golden Wedding year in 2001. Children Penelope 1955, Andrew 1957.

Served Tanganyika, East Africa 1951/71 as Resident Engineer in the Electrical Supply Industry at Morogoro, Arusha and Mwanza. Hon Consul British High Commission 1961/71. Ex Golf Club Captain Morogoro and Yacht Club Commodore Mwanza. I am an invited member of the Tanganyika Golfing Society and a Hon Life Member of the Mwanza Yacht Club.

I retired from East Africa in 1971 and became licensee in the Red Lion, Meliden, North Wales 1971/1988.

I enjoy reading, golf and mountaineering and the occasional pipe, pint and cigar. I started writing short stories in 1988 with limited luck, and poetry in 1996 from which I have achieved some success.

My poetry is self-taught as is my typing and which I consider broad church with no specific avenues, although I tend to be more cynical than serious but I can give clout when I feel it justified. I think Remus House has given me more encouragement that I truly deserve.

Two Score Years And Ten

A long time ago I went to a dance
        it was there I met Jeannie, of course, just by chance,
it was love at first sight, I fell for her style
        and some three years later we walked down the aisle.

All through our long courtship I was working at sea
        as a ship's engineer in the Merchant Navy,
this kind of arrangement wasn't one of the best
        but our separation stood up to the test.

Two children we had to make up the crew
        first there was Penny and then came Andrew,
and now they are married with four lovely kids
        all growing, and healthy and very kindred.

Soon after our wedlock, we found our eureka
        in the African county then called Tanganyika,
two decades we lived there, time we'll never forget
        the life and the sunshine and good honest sweat.

In this day and age, unions don't last too long
        just five or six years and then all has gone wrong,
so to celebrate fifty from such a weak start
        just proves it was true love, straight from the start.

How quickly they've gone, those past fifty years
        we've had ups and downs and the odd little tear,
and yet we're together through love and through pain,
        if I had my time over, I'd ask her again.

And now with this poem our story is told,
        we both keep on going, but daily grow old,
life hasn't been easy but it's all been worthwhile,
        all those short fifty years since we walked down the aisle.

BLACK FRIDAY

My Black Friday started with my getting up late
  which put my day's programme way out,
then the water went cold halfway through my bath
  and I started to limp through my gout.

I just missed my bus to take me to town
  thus making me late for my work,
my boss told me off so I gave him a thump
  all because he had called me a jerk.

The police were OK and the cell not so bad
  though the blanket had seen better days.
In front of the bench I was fined twenty quid
  and advised I should better my ways.

I arrived home that night, in my house couldn't get
  as my keys, in my case, were at work,
it was raining quite hard so a window I smashed,
  on the door, at the rear, near the kirk.

I'd no sooner got in, when the door bell did ring
  at the door of the house that I lease,
I then got a shock, for standing outside
  was a cop, from the local police.

'Caught you my lad,' he said with a smirk,
  'your presence in here rather smells,'
I tried to explain, but what could I say
  and I spent a cold night in the cells.

The fifty quid fine was for wasting court time
  with a warning that jail would be next.
then I went back to work to find I'd been sacked,
  as the boss I had hit was quite vexed.

Oh Happy Day

The other morn while having my shave
  with my face all covered with foam,
I smiled at myself, such a terrible sight,
  rather like a statue from Rome.

To my utter surprise my reflection smiled back
  which put my poor head in a spin,
gone was the frown that I usually see
  in its place was a cheeky broad grin.

I practised my smile many times on that day
  and each time the result was perfection,
smiling and grinning, such a difference it made
  what a joy just to see my reflection.

I went to the shop and tried out my smile
  on the girl who was usually quite grim,
to my pleasant surprise she returned it at once
  and her face was transformed with a grin.

The man next in line who was watching us both
  saw my smile and caught the infection,
then all down the queue people started to smile
  you'd have thought they'd received an injection.

All through the shop people started to smile
  one or two simply had a good laugh,
the smile I had brought now took over the place,
  all the shoppers and all of the staff.

Then outside the shop I continued to smile
  at the folks and the kids in the street,
they in turn passed it on to whoever they met,
  I had given the whole village a treat.

THE JOY OF CHILDREN

Excited children, looking, pointing,
  parents happy also keen,
watching waves advance, retreating,
  leaving sands washed sparkling clean.

Children flock around the donkeys
  begging for a chance to ride,
stroking, feeding, hugging, loving,
  lucky donkeys, so much pride.

Fairground busy, noise terrific
  lights and music fills the air,
candyfloss and ice-cream cornets,
  rollercoaster gives us all a scare.

Darkness gathers, children tired,
  parents sagging in their stride,
time for home and bed is calling,
  'Please, oh please, just one more ride.'

UPON REFLECTION

My reflection is one about nature
  of birds and beasts of the wild,
of fishes and whales of the ocean
  and what happens when our climate turns mild.

I get very cross about culling,
  of rhino and stags of that sort,
of the cranks paying money to shoot them,
  then claim it's a matter of sport.

I get angry when listening to Westminster,
  of committees that don't seem to work,
the place seems awash with oral garbage
  and where leaders at times, go berserk.

I'm disgusted with some of our farmers
  and the cruelty some do to their stock,
the repulsive conditions some beasts live in,
  would give decent people a shock.

About gases I get really worried,
  of the toxic we pump in the air,
with factories in countries just doing their own
  and their leaders who don't seem to care.

Another sad thing is our people,
  their outlook to wild creatures alive,
and the teaching of children what nature's about
  that all creatures need help to survive.

The start of world weakness is *uno,*
  so much talk and yet so little done,
world leaders who lead us to nowhere,
  their main weapon is still the big gun.

THE CYCLE OF LIFE

It happens to us all, this birth, life and death,
  life is the 'tween time before your last breath,
your life is in limbo at times with much sighing
  and while you are living, you're actively dying.

You were never asked if you wished to be born
  you're seeded to life from somebody's spawn,
then they leave you to fight for your pennyworth,
  and this is your lot, all the time you're on Earth.

Therefore living and dying are one of the same
  the difference it follows is only in name,
and if dying is living we're dead from the start,
  there is life's mystery, it's called living art.

So, living is dying, that's life's story told
  and when you are dead you will quickly go cold,
then into the Earth where you'll no longer turn,
  then recycling begins by the aid of the worm.

Hence the old saying of ashes and dust,
  that is your reward for living with trust,
but look on the bright side, you've drawn your last breath;
  it happens to us all, this birth, life and death.

LETTER IN A BOTTLE

Captain Ted, on an island, surrounded by sand,
  kept watching horizons in case help was on hand,
a glint in the water catches his wary old eye,
  he saw a corked bottle and he let out a cry.

He opened the bottle, washed up on the beach,
  inside was a paper in too far to reach,
so he smashed the old bottle and pulled out a note
  and fished for his specs from inside his coat.

'Please help. I'm marooned after sinking my ship,
  somewhere on the ocean, three days in the trip,
I'm south of the line that runs round the Earth
  and east of the one that gives new days a birth.'

'I'm hot and I'm hungry and very afraid,
  and waiting for someone to come to my aid.
The fishes are friendly and help me to thrive
  and a fresh water stream to keep me alive.'

Ted studied the writing, the date and the name,
  and noticed with horror his was one of the same,
this letter was one he had posted last year,
  now someone had added a devilish jeer.

'I regret very much I signed for that trip
  I'm marooned same as you and from the same ship,
if you hadn't got drunk we'd still be afloat,
  and you wouldn't have run into that larger steamboat.'

'Our boat, overloaded, just sank like a stone
  and into the sea the crew were all thrown,
and if by some chance I survive this abyss
  I promise you captain, I'll give you a miss.'

QUIZ KIDS

'Grandpa, can we ask a few questions?'
  my grandsons had caught me off guard,
I nodded, wondering what I was in for
  'Better hurry, for I'm off down the yard.'

'Do cauliflowers come from California?
  Do fishes drink H^2 or just 0?
Why do onions make our eyes water?
  Why is bread we eat made out of dough?'

Does the sun make those lovely sunflowers?
  Do snowballs belong to snowmen?
Are butterflies used to make butter?
  And who made the springs in Big Ben?'

The questions were asked by each cousin,
  each one crisp, as if from a text,
there was nowhere to go so I stood there,
  wondering what in God's name would come next.

'Are we going too fast for you, Grandpa?
  could we ask just a few questions more?'
I nodded my head in agreement,
  'Just be quick for my head is quite sore.'

'Do bluebottles live in blue bottles?
  Is the world's smallest bird called a wren?
If the world is round, why are there corners?
  Why is Japanese money called Yen?'

I was crushed by the speed of the questions,
  the boys knew it and gave a 'Ha Ha.'
'You thought you could answer these quizzes
  but you don't know much . . . do you Grandpa?'

THAT OTHER WOMAN

I have a special girlfriend,
  we meet most every day,
she's full of life and talkative
  and always wants to play.

She tells me of her boyfriends,
  the lads she's met somewhere,
our Peter seems her fancy most
  but he's too old to care.

She loves to eat, this lady friend
  and Smarties she loves most,
she is a very happy girl
  outgoing, without boast.

She's very bright, this friend of mine
  and sometimes comes for tea,
her memory's quite amazing
  for a lass of only three.

She rarely is a naughty girl
  doing things she shouldn't oughta,
she is a gal that's full of life,
  she's Natalia, my grand-daughter.

Tony King

I started life as the youngest of four children and I am now the oldest of three. My two older step-brothers and sister all died in their thirties. However, twins, Karen and Adrian were born in 1965 and thankfully they are still around.

My interest in writing goes back to when I was nine years old. I wrote a song. It was simple, and looking back not very good, but it was a start. Since then I have written many.

I made a promise to myself that I would be a published author by the time I was forty years old and just managed to achieve that with a poem, coincidentally in an anthology published by Forward Press. Since then I have had others published and placed equal third in an International Library of Poetry competition. As far as other writing goes, I have written a novel entitled *Minstrel,* which I would like to see published. If any publishers or agents are interested?

I'll have a go at virtually anything, if it means I will gain experience from it. I look at all the people I meet, things I see and stories I hear as ammunition; fuel for my writing. That's how it should be, experience it, feel it, share it.

The selection of poems I have chosen, span my life to date and underline the sentiment of the previous paragraph. I hope you enjoy sharing them with me.

FIRST BLOOD

A football game with Grandad,
At Cleethorpes by the sea.
Me three years old and awkward,
Him nearly seventy.

He kicks, stiff legged, flat cap on.
On gravel loose I chase.
I fall, legs straight up in the air.
My head lands first, 'sans grace'.

'There's blood, that's going to need a stitch.'
My father's tone was grave.
'We'll take him down to the St John's.
Now lad, you'd best be brave.'

St John's could not do stitches,
To Grimsby we did fly.
Me losing blood from gaping wound.
I knew that I would die.

Of course, there was no need to fret.
A minor wound, soon healed.
I still can feel the little knot,
The doctor tied and sealed.

BRIAN

The man who played with my train set,
stood tall in Army shoes.
The father of my two nieces and young nephew.
The oldest of my father's sons,
a stepbrother to me.
A role model of how I could,
or should turn out to be.

When Army calling left him,
to 'civvies' first reserve.
He turned to plumbing, heating,
made himself a new career.
A semi in the suburbs,
a wife, three kids, a life.
A few beers and a laugh,
down at 'The Arkle', Friday nights.

But discipline called to him,
the Army had a hold.
He trained for Prison Service,
but took bad with a cold.
The oldest of my father's sons,
a stepbrother to me.
Died Christmas Day,
Nineteen seventy-one
aged only thirty-three.

11 ASTON ROAD

Mum told me Grandad had died.
He had been ill for quite some time.
That staring, blank senility.
No life, no function left to see.

We could not tell his wife, Grandma.
She'd had a stroke, but seemed alright.
Four wards between his death her life.
Though neither knew each other's plight.

Sunday that week, she joined her spouse.
Another stroke, this time with no reprieve.
Within six days they both were taken from our lives.
Fortunate for us, we knew just how to grieve.

Gone were the days that I would visit Aston Road.
Number eleven, Gran and Grandad's terraced home.
Another chapter in my life had ended there.
I locked the door and swallowed back a final tear.

KEEP MOVING

A noise, what's that?
They've found me,
too soon, too soon.
Keep moving, double back.
Take to trees,
to leave no track.
Cross a stream, their dogs confuse.
Empty bins of ripe refuse.

No rest, no sleep.
Keep moving.
No more, no more.
Give in, give out.
Too much at stake,
I have to prove
they cannot break.
Think clever moves,
to shake them off.
They're getting close,
don't even cough.

I hide, can't breathe,
my lungs burn.
The pain, the pain.
Keep moving.
No just freeze,
keep still.
They'll find you now,
or never will.
They've gone confused.
Now time to rest,
I think I might just pass this test.

FIREWORK DISPLAY

Darkness of eternal gloom,
filling my mind quite slowly.
Drowning in a sea.
A grey, slow end eternity disguised.
Choking me inside.

Then, like a cold sharp cry.
Bursting like a shell,
it filled the sky.
Lighting up the corners of my mind.
Shining so that I may never die.

Gone again.
And left behind a sea of minds
that thought of light.
Touched with second sight.
So bright to dim the night.
A firework display.

BYRON (A CAT AN' A HALF)

They say that things in black and white,
are clear and safe and true.
Well I'll agree with all of that,
but nothing was safe with that darn cat.

He'd scratch my feet when late I slept,
and pounce on dogs that passed.
Sit quietly upon my knee,
Then scratch my hands and quickly flee.

One time, when thieves had dropped a haul,
of spirits in the street.
He'd paused to lap the liquor rough,
jumped on the ledge then fallen off.

He'd sit upon the terraces,
at Bramley Rugby League.
On match days a familiar sight,
was Byron, cat, in black and white.

Yes, Byron was a plucky cat,
so full of character.
Such personality and charm,
to keep him safe and free from harm.

He didn't come home one foul night,
I waited up and searched.
The next day, all ill thoughts denied.
I found him stiff, the road beside.

LADY OF THE MANOR

The Lady of the Manor has passed on.
The ambulance arrived, she could not wait.
Her mother and her brother watched in disbelief.
The body bag removed the Lady late.

Police and others asked them questions of her state of mind.
But difficult they found such truth to take.
How could she choose a Thursday morn to end her life?
No, someone must have made a big mistake.

Her brother went to tell their younger sister too.
The Lady's children also he must tell.
Stephen was eleven, David five, but Robert knew.
He was thirteen and going through such hell.

Her other brother came home from his holiday.
Two thirty in the morning, in a tired state.
The presence of his older brother worried him.
It wasn't long before he too had heard her fate.

The lady was my sister, Susan was her name.
I look back often now and always wonder why.
What weakness stopped her telling us, how bad she felt?
And where did she find the strength to choose to die?

THE TRUTH WITHIN

Turning my pencil with rhythm and sway.
The story it's telling are more words to say.
A picture unfolding in charcoal and white.
Whatever remains it will please me tonight.

Many like you will be leaving today.
And nothing could ever induce them to stay.
They're off to discover the people they've lost.
The truth that's within has a strange kind of cost.

Turning my pencil, imagine it dance.
Whilst leaving a trail full of life and romance.
The paint and the pastel add colour delight.
Whatever remains it will please me tonight.

Many like me have so much left within.
It fights for release, till you can't hold it in.
And when it breaks free so few do understand.
The truth that's within turns a child to a man.

RIVER RUNNING

When it's so late that it's early and I cannot find my sleep.
And my mind's a running river, twisting, turning, getting deep.
Let me take you by that river, let us listen to its sound.
As we walk we'll hear it singing, soothing voices all around.

Memories of springtime days that ever echo in the mind.
Everywhere there is renewal, everywhere a song to find.
But I always fall returning with a jolt into my room.
I'm alone and far from paradise, immersed in endless gloom.

True love always comes, unlooked for, gliding down on silent wings.
Sends you sprawling on the hard earth, joy and misery it brings.
Tangled up with your emotions, love will struggle to break out.
Though it hurts, shows no compassion, it would hurt you more without.

When a tear falls from a lover, as the pain exceeds the fear.
See it fall into the river, ripples silently appear.
Then it's gone, part of the deluge, twisting, turning, getting deep.
Leaves its stain upon my pillow, as I fight to find my sleep.

ANOTHER WATERFALL

I am a waterfall.
Just another waterfall.
You watch my life cascade,
down rocks and stones I've made.
Each drop of water clear,
are seconds when you're near.
Come hear my soothing call,
another waterfall.

I know the first I'm not,
and some seen are at once forgot.
And waterfalls you've seen,
in many places you have been.
So won't you listen to my song,
the one that I sing all day long.
The one song that for me is all,
another waterfall.

For there are days when no one hears my cries,
and there are clouds above me in the skies.
And all my tears flow down this rocky side,
but no one sees them, in this waterfall they hide.

Don't turn away from me.
Lie down here close and rest.
The riddle that I ask,
the answer you have guessed.
For every lonely heart,
there is a name to call,
and all their tears they start,
another waterfall.

FROM WHERE I STAND

From where I stand, I see his view.
Something I thought I'd never do.
But now I've reached the age he'd gained,
When first I knew him, all's explained.

For now I see the wisdom clear,
That battered once my childhood ear.
And those forgotten warnings, threats.
A thousand little epithets.

But proud was I of my strong dad.
The hardest any ever had.
No one would dare to cross or cuss,
The man who cared for all of us.

Such hurt a son will never know,
Of Father's worries, till they grow.
And when their children, trouble make.
Give the advice they'd never take.

From where I stand I see him clear.
He's smiling now, I feel him near.
Whenever I speak to my lad,
I hear his voice, his words, my dad.

THE FIRST DAY OF MY LIFE

Though all the stars were shining, not all the worlds were read.
A chapter new unfolded, dried the tears that I had bled.
Looking down from Sgurr Nan Gillean at Loch Slapin's deepest blue.
'Twas the morning of the first day of my life that led to you.

Like young Wallace proud and dauntless, I drove southwards
                                                  from the Glen.
Vanquished all who stood before me, full of life and strength again.
Standing tall, in silence waiting, for the love I felt was due.
'Twas the daytime of the first day of my life that led to you.

Herald cries and fanfares blasted, celebrations all around.
When the spirit least expects it, that is when a love is found.
In the midst of white tailed eagles, was an angel fair and true.
'Twas the evening of the first day of my life that led to you.

Still, not all the words are read, but that is how the work should flow.
Never ends the living story, where it's going we don't know.
Where it leads me I will follow, what it asks of me I'll do.
'Tis still only just the first day of my life that led to you.

Paul McIntyre

I was born on 22 April 1977 (I've just gone twenty-four) in Marsden Hudds. I was raised by my mother and grandmother, and I've never known my father. I was raised strict Catholic and went to a Catholic school. I was an altar boy for my Holy Family Slathwaite Church. Though I don't go to church now I am still religious.

I realised I was homosexual when I was very young, but knew I couldn't help how I felt. I told people around me when I was fifteen and got a mixed reaction. I started to write down my feelings and dreams on paper. Poetry is my escape from the pressures of life.

I think people of all ages can relate to my poetry. I cover most issues, and lots of my poems hold a special message. There's a poem for everyone in my collection and my poems can be interpreted in different ways.

I would like to become a famous poet and also take my poetry to theatre and do poetic plays etc . . . with background music. My poems would make interesting scenes/costume. I think so much more can be done with poetry than writing it. It's artistic and versatile. A lot of my poetry is still the insecure child in me, but as I learn more and more each day eventually my poetry will excel and become more real - maybe!

For me poetry is the most deep way of expressing my inner self. So much so that at times only yourself can understand it. But one poem to one person can be a different one to somebody else with a different meaning and message.

In the future I'd like to do charity books.

INTRODUCTION

Poems for all young and old
From fairytales to nature
Poems of love, both warm and cold
And stories of our Creator
Poems for loved ones passed away
Whom we all dearly miss
Poems about Wars of today
Poems sealed with a kiss
Memories, happy and sad
Tears with a dream
Times endured, good and bad
Folk not what they seem
These poems may make you laugh or cry
They may also help you cope
As they bring a tear to your eye
You may find some words of hope
Everyone of us are a moment in time
And sometimes we depart
We all have thoughts and I've shared mine
In poems from the heart

RAINBOW

After the sun came the showers
In the stream I saw waters flow
Pouring over pretty flowers
And now I see a big rainbow

On the other side, I've been told
I could find some hidden treasure
Some silver or a pot of gold
Hidden amongst deep green heather

I see the dew fall on the hills
As its sparkle catches my eye
And through the rocks the water spills
All underneath the sun-drenched sky

A moment like this is so rare
With magic colours in the air.

HE MADE OUR WORLD

He made our world, the King of Kings
I sing His praise, I sing His hymns.
I drink the wine, I eat the bread
It was our sweet Jesus who bled
Jesus performed such marvellous things

In the church I confess my sins
And pray for love that Jesus brings
From the Chalice we'll all be fed
He made our world.
For us He made wonderful things
For birds to fly He made their wings
Each night before I go to bed
I think of all the Bible said
He made our world.

PANTOMIME ACT

This life is like one big pantomime act
Where the different characters take their lead
Yet there still seems much fiction than fact
It's a play where we all want to succeed

The play falters and the acting gets worse
Yet still there seems to be so much applause
There are torn scripts people didn't rehearse
And people are walking through the wrong doors

To making money there seems no limits
A real life play that is not going right
Counting the days, I'm counting the minutes
Still there are people who need the spotlight

As people deceive, they're playing the fool
For sake of the camera they want to rule

NEVER FAR

You are as happy as a lark
As stars are shining just for you
Your angel is playing her harp
You are blessed with luck through and through

Your skies are as blue as can be
There will never be a dull cloud
The birds will whistle happily
Your voice of joy still sings out loud

Your loveliness will always reign
You will always be looked after
Your sunny meadows shall remain
With the echoes of your laughter

For I know wherever you are
Your joyful soul is never far

FREE SPIRIT

Her soul is shining
Full of love
Her spirits climbing
Up above
To the heights
Where no man's been
Seeing sights
We've never seen
Like from a dream
Though oh so real
She now can touch
All we can't feel
Don't cry too much
You're not apart
Though you can't see her
She's in your heart

CRYSTAL SKIES (CRYSTAL WATERS)

Ice shall freeze over the river
A warm sun will no longer rise
Leaves upon the trees shall wither
And all because of crystal skies

Sheets of cold glass will cover lakes
The air will become cold and cruel
Grass will be hidden by snowflakes
And frozen shall be every pool

All the flowers will become lost
Where a blanket of whiteness lies
And everything shall turn to frost
And all because of crystal skies

Everything that nature brought us
Will freeze around crystal waters

WATER WILL RUN

Waters will run, fires will flare
The sun will rise, the rain shall pour
Fog will cover the shallow air
While sands will still cover the shore

There's mountains snow will fall upon
And a forest with a reindeer
There's fountains where waters fall from
All this nature will remain here

A shooting star darts through the night
And it is darting fast and free
A place so far birds take their flight
A House Martin flies happily

Nature may not drown out sorrow
But helps us pull through tomorrow

YOU ARE

You are my diamond in the light
You are my ruby glowing red
You are my candle burning bright
You are the silk upon my bed

You are my stone that's made of gold
You are my emerald shining green
You are the one I need to hold
The most precious thing I have seen

You are my very own precious jewel
You are my sapphire shining blue
And I know you are the one who'll
Make all of my dreams become true

Everything special that I see
Is everything you are to me

MEMORIES

Let us not waste time dwelling on the past
as it's now time for me to look ahead
Those precious days went by extremely fast
but we'll now look to the future instead

Still when looking back, my heart grows fonder
Yes, I still see that twinkle in your eye
Oh the years gone by I'll always ponder
A special candle's flame can never die

With a secret shared, a heart is broken
I hear a careless whisper in the wind
There's thoughts of sorrow with cruel words spoken
I'm lighting a candle for I have sinned

Is there a memory you can't let go
That is portraying happiness and woe.

A Summer's Day In June

Turtle doves, flamingos and swans
With glorious colours of green
Bluebirds sing their beautiful songs
By a blue and glittering stream
Also there are butterflies too
Hovering over the flowers
All underneath the skies of blue
Casting their mystical powers

Through scented meadows we both walk
The day is so sunny and grand
We don't feel any need to talk
Just breathe in true love hand in hand

I shall never forget this year
In those such pretty summer days
I'll remember the way we were
Across the field two lovers gaze

A summer's day to remember
But summer days will pass so soon
In six months it will be December
And gone will be the month of June
So today I will surrender
To this wonderful afternoon
With days I will hold so tender
With all the flowers in full bloom

A very special summertime
As I am yours and you are mine

MAGICAL WORLD

Somewhere there is a wonderland
In a far away place beyond
When you're asleep in slumberland
A fairy casts her magic wand

A place that's hard to understand
As nothing seems to make much sense
Fairies and gnomes stand hand in hand
A world of magic and suspense

A princess named Cinderella
Who wed a rich and caring prince
He's a strong and handsome fella
They have been happy ever since

As she escaped the wicked queen
Snow White became a princess too
And now she's living out a dream
A fairytale made for two

A different world up a beanstalk
Or down a fancy rabbit hole
A place where animals can talk
You'll feel the magic in your soul

A place of magic and of peace
A place where wonders never cease

STARLET

Life a manufactured robot
Or like a puppet that's on strings
Riches and glamour but for what?
You are the china doll that sings.

You're now on show, it's time to smile
You are the actor, just pretend
Your life is joyful - never vile
But do you have a loyal friend?

You'll see the world for how it is
What is loved is your illusion
You're not your own as you are his
Just an object of confusion.

You play your part and play it well
A perfect life, or living hell?

Can we envy from a distance when
Things aren't always as they seem.

FORGIVE AND FORGET

Presents all each with a ribbon
Those things we said we'll now forget
All we said is now forgiven
We should no longer feel upset

Starting new, we'll cast our shadows
And help to let the light shine through
And to us, whatever life throws
You have got me and I've got you

We have to turn ourselves around
Painting new colours for the day
Our love was lost but is now found
It's time we were to find our way

The light of love will always shine
I want you to always be mine.